MW00916258

rest

A
NEUE THING
STUDY

COLLAGES
CAROL ANN WAGNER, carolannwagner@email.com, @cawstudio

All quoted Scripture (unless otherwise noted) is from:

DEDICATION

To my mom, who raised me to first know and love Jesus and to then know and love people well—you are a shining example of the love of Jesus Christ to everyone you encounter. My words on these pages are but an overflow of everything that you have taught me and modeled for me. May they bless others just as you have blessed me. I love you.

To my mother-in-law, who raised my favorite human being on this planet and did a fine job of it—thank you for faithfully serving the Lord, Dad, Chad, Heidi, and Jeremy all these years. You delight in bringing others joy through the work of your hands, and this world is a better place because of your presence. I love you.

CONTENTS

ABOUT
THE AUTHOR

 Cherie Wagner's life-long passion is two-fold: knowing Jesus Christ and making Him known. Author of *Found On My Knees* and *Awake O Sleeper*, Cherie desires to continue writing Bible studies for women that will encourage them to know and believe God's Word, equip them to live it, and empower them to take it and transform this generation for Jesus Christ. She writes, she speaks, and she teaches God's Word every opportunity that she can. Cherie and her husband, Jeremy, live in Phoenix, Arizona, where they are both actively involved in the ministries of Central Christian Church. Born and raised in Chicago and transplanted to the desert of Arizona, Cherie is a city girl at heart with a wild love for the mountains. A coffee connoisseur, a lover of knowledge, and forever a student of God's Word, she loves life and tries to live it to the fullest. Above all, she desires for this to be true of her life:

"But I do not account my life of any value nor as precious to myself, if only I may finish my course and the ministry that I received from the Lord Jesus, to testify to the gospel of the grace of God."

Acts 20:24

Connect with Cherie at **NeueThing.org**

YOU'RE INVITED
INTRODUCTION TO REST

I've learned something about myself this year. Actually, I think it's something that I may have always known, but perhaps I never really paid any attention to it. It's not necessarily a fun fact, nor is it something that I'm proud of, but here it is.

I have a hard time resting.

I feel a constant need to go and do and accomplish and work. Margin is difficult for me. Sabbath is hard. It shouldn't be, but it is. Even as I read the words I just typed, I find that they sound odd because while it is hard for me to rest, I know that rest is one of my greatest needs. I'm not great at creating margin in my life, but I'm increasingly aware of my need for it.

And I'm not talking about sleep, as wonderful as that can be. It's so much more than that. The kind of rest I'm referring to is a quieting of the noise of life which results in an awakening of the soul, a coming alive to the presence of our Creator, and an increased awareness to even the faintest whispers of His voice.

Busyness drowns out the still voice of God, the voice that is beckoning us to come and inviting us to rest. When the pace of our lives is a constant running from one thing to the next, we tragically miss the invitation. But don't miss it now.

"Come to me, all you who are weary and burdened, and I will give you rest."

Matthew 11:28

When we lack margin, "weary and burdened" are just around the corner. When we find ourselves bowing down to the constant demands of our schedules more than we are bowing down to Christ, God's voice is no longer the loudest voice in our lives. And that, my friends, is a dangerous place to be. Trust me, I've been there.

Just as I have heard His invitation afresh, calling me to set down my tasks and schedules and meetings and to-do lists in order that I might find rest for my soul, His invitation is extended to you today, as well. Don't miss it.

Come rest. Lay your burdens down, and find all that you need in His presence. The heavy weight of responsibility that you've been carrying that pushes you to keep going, never allowing you for one moment to pause and take a breath—lay it down.

You're invited.

Come, find rest in the One who created it.

To all who are weary, to everyone who is burdened, fellow sojourner: Today, you're invited to lay down your heavy loads and find rest for your souls. For just a moment, position yourself in His presence. Sit at His feet. Drink from His river. Graze in His pasture. Feast from His table. Rest in His embrace. You'll be so glad you did.

DAY 1
GOD RESTED

I don't know about you, but I have always loved the story of creation as recorded in the book of Genesis. Even from the time I was a child, I have been fascinated with this miraculous account of God speaking all that I can see into existence. I can vividly remember the flannel graphs used in Sunday school, and I can picture even now in my mind the images used nearly thirty years ago to depict this story.

For the first five days of creation, God used words alone to form and create the world. That is just baffling to me! There is such a display of God's power recorded within the first few chapters of Genesis. He opened His mouth and said, "Let there be …," and then there was. He didn't even need to use His hands to create. His word was all that was necessary. His Word is still all that we need.

Then we get to day six in the creation story, the day on which God decided to create mankind. You can read about this in Genesis 1:26-31 and again in Genesis 2:4-25. What has always stood out to me the most in this part of the story is that on day six, God decided to use His hands. Notice how every day of creation, God spoke things into existence. Only on man did He use His hands.

That, my friends, is an intentional, loving God, a God who is not distant, but a God who gets involved in the details of our lives. He knelt down, got His hands in the dirt, and breathed life into us.

Here's where I want us to fix our gaze today, though. On day seven, God chose to rest. Breathe that in for just a moment. It's beautiful. Read these few verses below:

"Thus the heavens and the earth were finished, and all the host of them. And on the seventh day God finished His work that He had done, and He rested on the seventh day from all His work that He had done. So God blessed the seventh day and made it holy, because on it God rested from all His work that He had done in creation." Genesis 2:1-3

Before we take one step further, it is critical to note that God didn't rest because He was tired. God is God, and He is not confined by the limitations of man. God does not grow tired or weary as we do. God does not need to take a nap. God doesn't take breaks from ruling and reigning over all of creation. He is God.

Still, I know that God is intentional in all that He does, so I believe that His choice to rest was also very intentional. I imagine you could come up with your own reasons as to why God chose to rest on the seventh day, but allow me to submit two reasons of my own.

Why did God choose to rest?

1

. . . .

God rested in order to model for us what we should also do.

God wasn't tired, but He knew we would be. He knew the importance of ceasing work for just a day to revive and restore our weary souls. He knew the necessity of moving away from the demands and pressures that work brings for just one day in order that we might regain our focus on Him. He desired this for us, so He modeled it for us. The beauty of the God we love and serve is that in all matters of obedience, He showed us how to do it.

2

. . . .

God rested to reflect on all that He had just created.

He had just spent six days hard at work creating the universe. So, He took a day to reflect on all He had made. Again, God is modeling for us the importance of rest. There seems to be this never-ending drive within humanity to keep going, to work harder, to never stop. However, a day of pause and reflection can serve us so well. When we stop to reflect on the work we've accomplished, there is not only pleasure and joy to be found, but there is also the ability to regain perspective. *"Was all the hard work worth it? At what cost was I able to accomplish it all? Would I do anything differently?"* When we rush from one day to the next, eliminating rest in the grind to accomplish more, we remove these benefits from our lives.

If there were no other reason given to us to rest than the fact that God chose to do it Himself, that would be enough. It is wisdom to imitate God. That is what we are called to do as followers of Jesus Christ. In all things, imitate God as beloved children. So, are we?

My conviction from Day 1:

....

....

....

....

....

....

....

....

....

....

My prayer:

....

....

....

....

....

....

....

....

....

....

DAY 2
FROM ADRENALINE TO EXHAUSTION

I want to invite you to just ponder both of those words before we go much further.

Adrenaline.

Exhaustion.

At first glance, they may seem like polar opposites or strikingly different extremes. However, after deeper reflection, I can't help but wonder if there is a fine line between the two, a very fine line that perhaps we have been tiptoeing on for too long.

"Come with me by yourselves to a quiet place
and get some rest."

Mark 6:31b

For quite some time now, Jesus has been wooing me to places and spaces of rest. While that might sound extraordinary to some, it really had become a bit of a foreign concept to me. Rest seemed to fall somewhere on the back burner of the more pressing or urgent issues in life and ministry, and needless to say, I had fallen out of the discipline of solitude and rest.

One can only go so long before "running on fumes" doesn't cut it anymore. Jesus knew this, and He taught His disciples to know this first-hand. In Mark 6:31b, we read of Jesus' very personal invitation to His closest friends to retreat with Him and get some rest. The disciples had just finished a rather intense and demanding season of ministry alongside Jesus, and they had spent an extended amount of time pouring themselves out for the sake of others.

I intentionally left out the first half of Mark 6:31 until now to make a point. If you don't already have your Bible open, grab it, and flip it open to Mark 6:31. Now, read the verse in its entirety.

Then, because so many people were coming and going that they did not even have a chance to eat, He said to them, "Come with me by yourselves to a quiet place and get some rest."

I don't have to wonder at whether or not you and I have found ourselves in a similar place. The pace of life has quickened so much (or we have allowed it to), that there are days when we literally have left no margin or time to physically feed ourselves. I mean, literally. Our days are packed full of running here and doing that, meeting with so-and-so, appointments and soccer practices … chasing, chasing, chasing, and never resting. I'm not even talking about a nap, although the Lord knows how much some of us need one. I'm referring to a refreshing of our souls, one that can only come from time spent in God's presence. Time spent in prayer. Time spent with Jesus, sitting at His feet, soaking up every word, just like Mary did, while Martha ran and ran trying to do and do.

Rather, we live much of our lives from this frantic place of adrenaline, hoping that the steam doesn't wear off until that final task or obligation has been completed. Then we crash, and sometimes burn, only to get up the next day and somehow manage to do it all over again. Instead of this less than desirable dwelling in the frantic, could we take a moment and consider Jesus' personal invitation to us today?

He invites us to put down the busy in order to pick up retreat with Him and grab some rest—some much needed rest—for our souls. He calls us out of the stress and the pressures of life to regularly and repeatedly be with Him. Again and again and again. Not just on Sunday mornings. Not just at mid-week Bible study. Every moment of every day. Do we take Him up on His offer? Do we prioritize refreshment? Or do we keep putting it off, thus depleting our very souls one day, one hour, and one minute at a time?

I don't know about you, but I don't want to burn out. And as much as there are things to get done, and my own "to do" list seems to keep growing with each passing moment, I have learned to come to the river of God when I'm thirsty and to run to His Word when I'm in need of strength. When I feel the adrenaline kicking in, I know it's probably been a bit too long since I retreated and rested with my King.

Are you in need of some rest today, friends? Jesus is calling.

"Come with me by yourselves to a quiet place and get some rest."

Mark 6:31b

My conviction from Day 2:

....

....

....

....

....

....

....

....

....

....

My prayer:

....

....

....

....

....

....

....

....

....

....

DAY 3
PSALM 62

For nearly 365 days of the calendar year, I find myself under blue skies. Typically, there isn't a cloud in the sky, and the sun shines brightly. I can imagine most of you drooling right now. What you would give for such a climate to call home, right? Well, one important thing I've left out of this equation is that the temperatures range in the triple digits for about 5-6 months a year. You begin to understand an entirely new level of the word "hot" when you live in the desert.

Still, there are those rare but occasional days when the sun sinks behind a cloud, the sky is gray, and if we're lucky, we'll even see some rain. These happen to be my most favorite days, because they are so few and far between. They present themselves as a bit of a reprieve from the harsh heat that defines most of our days. It's like a much needed break, a retreat. For me, it's rest.

Today was one of those days. In the middle of the summer, when we typically boast our highest temperatures, I'm sitting outside in pants and a long-sleeved shirt, not sweating a drop. This is what I like to call good. On days like today, I find it easy to connect with God. I see Him in the cloudy skies, and I experience Him in the cooler breeze. It's when the pavement is hot and life seems even hotter that my natural default moves away from Him and onto other, lesser things.

This is what I love about Psalm 62. King David finds himself in the heat of life within these twelve short verses, and although he uses some of this space to talk about the struggle, he sandwiches his pain with praise. He reflects on who God is and on His faithfulness, and it is that alone that sees him through.

Notice in verse one:

"Truly my soul finds rest in God; my salvation comes from Him." (NIV)

Notice again in verse five, as if he hasn't even skipped a beat:

"Yes, my soul, find rest in God; my hope comes from Him." (NIV)

Still, in between these two professions of faith, we read his words of desperation and despair. Here's the truth of it all. David could have chosen to remain in the place of verses three and four, but he didn't. He began from a place of praise and recognition of who God is, he came back to that place in the middle of his refrain, and he landed the plane there at the end. I love this about David because it reveals his humanity. He was no greater than you or I. He was a flawed, broken, weak individual, one who was daily and desperately in need of God's grace. Just like you. Just like me. So, he talked about the real, unfortunate, and painful things of his life, but he always brought the conversation back to praise.

And don't miss this, friends: This is what secured his rest.

Notice, it wasn't will power on his part or sheer determination to overcome the mountains that faced him. It was his choice to recognize who God was. It was his default which proclaimed that God was his source of salvation and hope, not his circumstances nor his ability to overcome them.

He repeats himself again in verses two and six when he declares to all what is the firm foundation upon which he stands.

"Truly he is my rock and my salvation; he is my fortress, I will never be shaken." (NIV)

As I read these words this morning and look out over the gray skies that hover above me, I'm reminded of what true rest really looks like. It's not about managing or controlling my circumstances in order to ensure safety or comfort for myself. It's all about recognizing who God is despite my circumstances. Do you see the difference? We forfeit rest for our souls when we refuse to default to praise and instead rehearse the pain.

If we could choose our perspective today to be one that reflects trust in an unchanging, ever-faithful God, imagine the possibilities. We could renew our strength. We could soar on wings like eagles. We could run and not grow weary. We could walk and not be faint. (Isaiah 40:31) If we would but recognize where our hope comes from, rest would be our reality right around the corner.

My conviction from Day 3:

....

....

....

....

....

....

....

....

....

....

My prayer:

....

....

....

....

....

....

....

....

....

....

DAY 4
HOW THE EXCESS IS STRANGLING US

If I were to ask you, "What does the word 'margin' mean to you," how would you respond? Would you immediately think of the spacing that lines the edges of your documents in Microsoft Word? Or, would you go a bit deeper in contemplation, thinking about the importance of boundaries and reserving time and space for yourself to rest?

This idea that the excess is strangling us has really hit home for me this past year. When I write and teach, I most often prefer to get right to the point, right to the meat of the passage of Scripture that I'm covering that day. However, there is need for personal stories and testimonies of what God has done in our lives that encourage us to keep running our own race. So, if you would go with me there today, I promise you there is great significance and Biblical insight in what I'm about to share with you. Just five minutes of your time? Thanks, friends.

For those of you who know me or spend any amount of time with me on a weekly or even monthly basis, you would probably remember well that 2014 was NOT my best year health-wise. In fact, I was very sick nearly all twelve months of 2014, and to say it was challenging would be the understatement of the year. While I've heard that many people move to Arizona to escape their allergy problems, mine found me here. I never struggled with allergy issues in my life, to anything, but after a few years of desert living, I found that "allergy season" was more of a year-round thing for me.

It hasn't been uncommon for me to have multiple sinus infections each year because I have found it very difficult to keep my symptoms under control. By the end of 2014, I felt as if I had exhausted every measure to find and maintain health in this area of my life but without success. I can't even tell you how many times I've said, "I'm sick and tired of being sick and tired." Anybody else?

At the beginning of February 2015, my travels brought me back to my roots—to the beloved city of Chicago. I always enjoy going back to visit for many reasons, one of which is that my allergies always calm down when I exit the valley of Phoenix. While in Chicago, I found myself in conversation with one of my best friends about this new diet she and her husband were on, and I was fascinated by the results she was experiencing. Now, PAUSE for just a moment to hear me say:

"I don't do diets. I never have. I will never be a fan of them."

Seriously, I don't. I've always been rather healthy and close to the weight I want to be, so there was ZERO appeal for me to do this diet she was describing in order to lose weight. I was intrigued, however, by the possibility of how this might affect my allergy issues.

I had never even contemplated changing my diet to see if that would help decrease my symptoms. I'm not entirely sure why it had never occurred to me, but it hadn't. In all honesty, my decision to try it was not much more than, "Why not? Nothing else has seemed to work. I might as well at least try it." So, I did, and not with incredibly high expectations because, mind you, I had been to all the doctors, taken all the medications (even the all-natural ones), exhausted every measure (or so I'd thought), and nothing had changed.

So, for 30 days, I eliminated much from my diet—no grains, no processed sugars, no dairy. Good grief, right?! What on earth DID I eat? Fruits, vegetables, and meat (essentially). After one week, I was off all four of my daily allergy medications. For the remainder of the month (and this was during the worst time of the year for allergies: March in Arizona), I was medication free. Simply cutting out the excess, that which I enjoyed, but did not need, restored long-lost health to my body.

Why am I sharing all of this with you? First of all, I'm NOT sharing it so that you'll run out and sign up for the next fad diet out there. I'm NOT. I am, however, wanting to start a conversation about the excess in our lives. If you were to tell me two months ago that I was going to live without processed sugars, dairy, and all grains for 30 days, I would have laughed in your face, because I simply would not have believed I could do it. I have lived life believing that I "need" certain things, because I have taught myself to crave them.

When it comes to our relationship with Jesus Christ, I wonder how much we crave Him. And if we don't, could it be because there is so much "excess" in our lives, that there is no perceived need for Him? There have been few times in my life when I have truly felt hungry. Of course, I've boldly proclaimed on countless occasions, "I'm starving!" But really? I've never really known hunger. When I'm hungry, I eat, and to be honest, I often eat past the point of being full. I eat whatever I want without much regard to whether or not it's good for me. Never had I considered whether what I was feeding my body was actually the cause or the effect of how sick I was feeling for so long. If I was craving a donut, I would typically eat two. If I wanted chips, I'd eat nearly the whole bag. And the excess was strangling me.

Food might not be your thing, but something is. Something is constantly pulling you in the opposite direction of Jesus. Something is stealing your time, energy, emotion, and resources from fully offering them to Christ. Something is promising you fulfillment, but the more you run to it, the less it satisfies and the more you want it. Something. I don't know what it is for you. It could be Facebook. Maybe it's shopping. Perhaps it's coffee, alcohol, work, people. Do you notice how nothing in the above list is wrong in and of itself? These are all good things—in appropriate portions. It's when we over-indulge and prioritize any one of these things more than Jesus that we err.

There is so much excess in our lives. Too much food. Too many clothes. Too many TV shows. Too much social media. Too many appointments on the calendar. Too many commitments. Too much clutter.

And too little time for Jesus. If we can say at the end of the day that we did not have any time to get into God's Word, but we somehow found time to scroll through every social media app on our phones countless times, our priorities are misplaced. If, at the end of the day, we can say that there was no time for prayer, but we found time to talk about our problems (or other people's problems) with someone else over the phone, over coffee, over email or text, our priorities are misplaced. The reality is that we will always make time for that which is most important to us, and quite frankly, friends, and please hear this in love, Jesus has become unimportant in many of our lives simply based on how we spend our time.

It's not as if we have lack. We have too much. We are being strangled by the excess in our lives, and the greatest casualty of all is that Jesus has been squeezed out of our days. We have so much, and daily we keep wanting and craving more because we are so dissatisfied with what we do have. And yet Jesus stands at the door of each of our hearts and knocks, and too often we don't "find enough time in the day" to open that door to Him.

What excess in your life could you do without in order to place God back in His rightful place, in first place, in your life? What needs to go so that God can return? What could be sacrificed so that Christ can be worshiped? Just some "food" for thought today.

"Taste and see that the LORD is good; blessed is the one who takes refuge in Him. Fear the LORD, you His holy people, for those who fear Him lack nothing. The lions may grow weak and hungry, but those who seek the LORD lack no good thing."

Psalm 34:8-10

My conviction from Day 4:

....

....

....

....

....

....

....

....

....

....

My prayer:

....

....

....

....

....

....

....

....

....

....

DAY 5
SUFFICIENT GRACE

"But He said to me, 'My grace is sufficient for you, for my power is made perfect in weakness.' Therefore I will boast all the more gladly about my weaknesses, so that Christ's power may rest on me."

2 Corinthians 12:9

Simply put, it has been a challenging week—one of those weeks that seems to bear far more difficulty, uncertainty, and grief than you believe you can handle. I know you've been there. We all have. Life doesn't tend to warn us of the storms that will inevitably come, and what I've learned is that if I'm not deeply rooted in the truth of God's Word, I will easily be blown and tossed by the waves. Trials seem to enter my life in the form of a tidal wave at times, and if I'm not careful and intentional to stand firm upon truth, I'm simply no match for the storm.

Several years ago, God spoke the truth of His sufficient grace over my life, or what was left of it. Due to circumstances that were outside of my control coupled with poor choices I had made, what remained of my heart was not much more than a pile of brokenness and a heap of ashes. Still smoldering from the fire, Jesus reached down into those ashes with His healing hand and began to piece back together what had been shattered. As He mended what had been broken and as I learned to cooperate with Him in the process, I experienced His sufficient grace.

SUFFICIENT

adequate for the intended purpose; enough

GRACE

the freely given, unmerited favor and love of God

Choosing to call to mind His faithfulness toward me in my past was the obedience necessary for me these past several days to offer hope in the face of temptation to despair. That is what rehearsing God's faithfulness will do. It allows us to believe that because God was faithful in our past, He will remain faithful in our present and in our future.

One of the many lies that has deceived so many of us is that Christ is just not enough. From the pits of our pain, we cry out, *"This pain is too great. This difficulty is beyond the hope of repair. This relationship is past the point of reconciliation. This despair is too dark."* And God replies with a greater, more powerful word of truth: *"My grace is enough."*

In the face of unimaginable shame, grief, sorrow, despair, hopelessness, hurt, anger, and fear, we are daily met with the promise of His sufficient grace. The extent to which we focus on something determines its size in our minds. So we have a choice. We either focus on our circumstance, that which we have little to no power to change, or we focus on the beautiful face of Jesus. The more we focus on our problem, the bigger it becomes and the smaller Jesus seems in our minds. The more we fix our gaze on our Savior, the smaller our obstacle becomes.

I know I needed this reminder today. Did you? The God of all comfort, love, mercy, and truth meets you and me each and every day with His sufficient (enough) grace (favor). Enough favor. Sufficient grace. I pray that you and I can find rest for our souls in that reality today. I pray that we might find the courage, strength, and resolve to proclaim today, "Jesus, you are more than enough." And as those beautiful words of truth pass over our lips, may they bring healing to our souls.

Jesus, you are all that I need. You are more than enough. Your grace is sufficient for my every need. I run to you. I rest in you.

My conviction from Day 5:

....

....

....

....

....

....

....

....

....

....

....

My prayer:

....

....

....

....

....

....

....

....

....

....

"Come to me, all you who are weary and
burdened, and I will give you rest."

Matthew 11:28

DAY 6

Spend some time meditating on the passage and collage on the previous page. What do you see? What do you hear? Write a prayer of reflection below.

DAY 7
WHERE TRANSFORMATION OCCURS

I've heard it said before that while Jesus will always meet you where you are, He loves you too much to leave you there.

Transformation.

I've said on countless occasions to countless women at countless gatherings that although every follower of Jesus Christ met the Lord at the foot of the cross, we were never intended to stay there. In fact, He issues every believer this invitation to abundant life with His words in Luke 9:23:

"Whoever wants to be my disciple must deny themselves and take up their cross daily and follow me." (NIV)

Transformation.

The new life in Christ that we have been called into is all about transformation—momentarily, hourly, daily, weekly, monthly, yearly, one degree at a time, slowly becoming less like ourselves and more like our Jesus.

But what happens when it gets hard? What happens when obedience is painful? What do we do when the transformation that God is calling us to is costly? The common answer to this question, at least from what I've personally experienced and seen in others, is that we grow weary. Our knees grow weak from standing, and they hurt from time spent on them in prayer. Our hearts become heavy instead of hopeful. Our minds are exhausted instead of encouraged. We don't even know why we're surprised by any of this. Jesus did in fact warn us of the cost of being His disciple. He never promised us an easy life free from trial and pain. Still, we're worn out, tired of the pruning process, and ready to throw in the towel of striving toward obedience. Our feet are dirty and calloused from the long journey.

We need rest.

There's no question that we have indeed been called to follow in His footsteps. There's no question that we have been commissioned to carry our cross. There's no debating on the matter of obedience. These are the non-negotiables. But at the end of the day, when all is said and done, when our arms are tired from all the heavy lifting and our minds and hearts have reached their capacity, where does the transformation actually occur?

In His presence.

Not in our doing, but rather in His presence. We have allowed our finite, human limitations to project limitations on our infinite God. We've confused obedience with salvation, and forgotten that it is by grace through faith that we are saved. We've erased margin from our lives, therefore eliminating the discipline of rest. And it is in the rest that transformation occurs.

Take a moment to read Matthew 11:28-30.

What is the opening command that we receive from the very mouth of Christ?

Come to me, and find rest.

How is it, then, that we have confused His invitation "to rest" with our striving "to do?" His invitation to rest is really a veiled request for our very hearts. He's not after our hands, friends. He has two of His own, and He holds the entire universe in them. He wants our hearts. He wants our affections. He wants our energy. He wants our time. He wants our focus. He wants our attention. He wants our hopes and dreams. He wants our marriages and our children. He wants us, not what we can do for Him.

Transformation occurs in His presence when we come to Him, laying all else aside, recognizing that what is pressing and urgent to us is not moving Him or causing Him an ounce of stress or anxiety. He's got it under control. He just wants us to come. He invites us to rest.

When is the last time you did?

Transformation occurs in His presence. So, live in the nearness of it.

My conviction from Day 7:

....

....

....

....

....

....

....

....

....

My prayer:

....

....

....

....

....

....

....

....

....

....

DAY 8
WHAT IS YOUR DEFAULT MODE?

This question could honestly be answered in a number of ways, depending on the context. We all default to different things given different situations. Your default mode at work might be perfectionism, driving you to be a workaholic. Your default mode at home might be "couch potato," shutting your brain off and soaking up the tube. Your default mode in relationships might be people-pleasing, always trying to keep everyone else happy. And maybe not. Perhaps your default modes are a bit healthier than mine, or at least what they used to be. Either way, I want to pose this question to you today to get you thinking a bit deeper about your faith.

When it comes to being a Christ-follower, what is your default mode?

When crisis hits your life, your marriage, your home—do you default to prayer or anxiety? Better yet, when things are going well, when the good times are rolling, when all seems right in your world, do you still default to prayer because being found on your knees is your comfort zone? Think about it. Does God desire to function as a personal 911 operator in our lives, or does He long for daily communication from us as His children? What is your default mode?

When you're faced with a big decision, do you default to asking everyone under the sun what they would do, or do you default to the wisdom and counsel found in God's Word? Does it even cross your mind to search out His truth first, or do you elevate the wisdom and knowledge of man over His? What is your default mode? Better yet, in the daily, seemingly mundane decisions in life, do you consult God's Word, desiring to walk in wisdom, or do you default to determining your own course, presuming that you are the one who controls the small stuff, anyway? What is your default mode?

I found myself in the pages of the book of Daniel today, and although I've spent an immeasurable amount of time in this book of the Bible before, I came across something I had missed in times past. Daniel 6:10 records that in spite of the decree that King Darius had just made, forbidding prayer to anyone or any god other than himself, Daniel immediately went to prayer to the One true God for all to see. In the past, I always just chalked that one up to Daniel being some kind of super Christian, the kind who only knows courage and never fear. This is simply not the case, though. Daniel was painfully human, just as you and I are. He fell prey to the same temptations that you and I face. He was probably more afraid than we have ever been in our lives, facing the very real threat of death by lions. However, Daniel's default was prayer.

You see, Daniel's entire life had been spent in faithful pursuit of God, and he wasn't about to compromise that now. He had learned the practice of being found on his knees, in the good and the bad, so this was really no different. He chose prayer because that is what he always did. This was his default mode.

Can we say the same for ourselves? Do we default to prayer, or is it merely our lifeline when we find ourselves in crisis? Jesus desires our whole heart, not just a part. When we only run to God in times of need, He is nothing more to us than a genie in a bottle. God wants us to learn the practice of being found on our knees when the sun is shining and when the rain is pouring down. Why?

Because He always deserves our attention, affection, esteem, and praise. Always. So let's give it to Him.

"Do not be anxious about anything, but in everything by prayer and supplication with thanksgiving let your requests be made known to God."

Philippians 4:6

When I think about the absence of anxiety in life, my mind defaults to a few of these things: peace, calm, stillness, and REST. Prayer is the vehicle that brings us to these desired places. When our default is prayer, we know peace. We know calm. We know stillness. We know rest.

What is it that is keeping you on your feet and off of your knees today? Rest is found when we humble ourselves in prayer.

My conviction from Day 8:

....

....

....

....

....

....

....

....

....

....

My prayer:

....

....

....

....

....

....

....

....

....

....

DAY 9
A WELL THAT NEVER WILL RUN DRY

"Oh, the depth of the riches and wisdom and knowledge of God! How unsearchable are His judgments and how inscrutable His ways!"

Romans 11:33

It's hard to imagine never thirsting again, isn't it? Thirst will forever be a basic human need. Every morning when I wake up, I am parched, craving water, and run straight for the faucet. It almost seems as if it's been days since my last drink of water, even though it has only been hours. Life on this side of heaven will remain filled with all sorts of physical needs that will never fully be satisfied. We will continue to want and need all sorts of things until we take our final breath. It is the nature of life.

But then there is the soul. We were created for relationship with our Creator, and when that relationship is left untended, or worse, is non-existent, the pain of unmet longing and dissatisfaction is nearly unbearable. When tended to and nurtured in Christ's love, the soul experiences the unspeakable joy of true satisfaction, and what keeps us coming back for more is the depth of His matchless love, a well that never will run dry.

I don't know if this all sounds just a bit too good to be true. It might. The mountain of need you are facing today may cause you to wince with doubt at these faith-filled words. The overwhelming feelings of loss and heartache may cause you to want to run for the hills instead of run to His arms. I know each of us is coming to the pages of God's Word today from different places and spaces. Still, despite our differing circumstances, we serve a God who does not change. So,

For each one of you staring down a difficult and seemingly impossible road ahead,

For the one who can hardly bear the thought of tomorrow,

For the one who has lost all hope for the future,

For the empty, dry, weary, and burdened sojourner,

For the defeated and tired,

Jesus invites you today to meet Him at the well, a well with waters that will never run dry; a flood for your soul that will leave you forever satisfied while causing you to run back for more of Him. Because the one who has tasted and seen that the LORD is good will never cease to dive into the depths of His river.

Maybe you have sought satisfaction, significance, worth, identity, and rest in everything but Jesus Christ. Today is the day to come to the Living Water and find rest for your soul. The riches and wisdom and knowledge of God will always surpass depths that we could even fathom. The more we come to know Him, the more we will want to know, and we'll never have it all figured out until we see Him face to face. My prayer for you today is that Jesus would absolutely thrill you as you seek Him. I pray that as you take that first trembling step of faith toward His open, loving arms, you would experience the depths of His love for you in just one embrace and that you would never turn back. As you purpose to fix your gaze on His face instead of your circumstances, may you find rest at His river.

My conviction from Day 9:

My prayer:

DAY 10
DESPERATE TIMES

"Thus says the LORD who made the earth, the LORD who formed it to establish it – the LORD is His name: 'Call to me and I will answer you, and will tell you great and hidden things that you have not known.'"

. . . .

Jeremiah 33:2-3

Desperate times call for desperate measures. Sound familiar? When was the last time you found yourself desperate? I mean truly desperate? Like, if God doesn't show up right now and somehow provide for your need, you just don't know how you will make it to tomorrow. I believe that times of desperation find us all. Not a single person on planet Earth is exempt from seasons of adversity. However, even the inevitability of those times doesn't necessarily produce within us a desperation for the Lord. It's sad, but true.

Let me explain. In our self-driven culture, we've grown far too self-sufficient, independent, and controlling, that we have forgotten what it looks like to truly rely on God as if our lives depended upon it. Maybe I should just speak for myself. I know that I have, in my selfishness, tried to meet my own needs and take care of myself instead of leaning on the Lord. Then, when the heat of the difficulty rises, I find myself scrambling to work things out, desperate for answers and solutions. Instead, shouldn't the attitude of my heart be one that defaults to relying on the Lord, being more desperate for His presence than for my need to be met? Both in the good and the bad times, shouldn't I be found "calling out to the LORD" as Jeremiah 33 instructs me to do?

My husband and I recently found ourselves in that place. The stress and pressures of life had caught up to us, and we were desperate. At first, we resorted to the bad habit of worry and fear. Isn't it so easy to do that? Make no mistake. You and I establish the bad habit of worry and fear by failing to remain and abide in Christ. We're not victims of fear. Fear is a choice. Whenever we are faced with something that seems beyond our control to fix, do we walk in fear or do we run in faith? After realizing that our worry was getting us nowhere fast, my husband and I hit our knees. We cried out to the LORD, desperate for Him to show up in our need and provide. His answer? He met us with His presence, with a fresh wave of His Spirit. He renewed our strength. He quieted our fears and strengthened our faith. Notice that our circumstance didn't necessarily change. Rather, our perspective did.

This is why He commands us to "call to Him." He is not suggesting that we think about it or even whisper it, but rather, the command given is to cry out to the God of Heaven and Earth, the One who spoke everything you see into existence. The One who breathed life into your lungs is more than able to sustain you in your time of need. Call out to Him. Be desperate for Him. He promises to answer, and in that, we find hope. We find a rest for our souls that self-sufficiency and determination cannot provide.

I am praying for you today that you will have faith to call out to the
LORD and believe that He is not only waiting to hear from you,
but He is also ready to answer you. I'm believing God that your
capacity to trust in the LORD will be increased beyond measure so
that you are ready and willing to rely on Him to meet your every
need. In this calling out to Him, in this newfound desperation and
dependency upon Him, may God grant you rest. May you know
peace. May you experience fullness of joy. May love overflow from
your life.

Remember, friends. The invitation still stands. Come and find
rest for your souls in the only One who can provide it. Call out to
Him. Lean into Him. Lay your heavy burden at His feet. Rest in
His arms.

My conviction from Day 10:

....
....
....
....
....
....
....
....
....
....

My prayer:

....
....
....
....
....
....
....
....
....

DAY 11
MY HOPE IS BUILT ON NOTHING LESS

"So shall my word be that goes out from my mouth; it shall not return to me empty, but it shall accomplish that which I purpose, and shall succeed in the thing for which I sent it."

Isaiah 55:11

There have been certain prayers that I have prayed for years, and many of these prayers I continue to pray without seeing an answer. At times I have felt persistent, and other times tremendously discouraged. Does God hear? Will He ever move in response to these prayers? Will I ever see results and change? Still, the command remains to never stop praying, and so I press on. I wonder if any of you feel this same way. Is there a prayer that you have prayed for longer than you can remember, waiting in eager expectation for God to answer, but you still find yourself in the waiting?

Rest is found while trusting God in the waiting.

For me, these ongoing, endless prayers are for my unsaved family members. I have prayed since I was a child and knew how to pray that all of my family would come to know Jesus. For years, I have shared my faith with them. From a young age, I can remember sitting across the table from my grandfather, telling him all that my young years knew and understood about faith, pleading with him to believe. Into my teens, I continued those conversations, repeatedly pointing back to God's Word as evidence to this unseen God. Into my twenties and now thirties, I have sat and listened and cried and boldly shared the hope of Jesus Christ with my brother, and still the waiting continues. For years, others in my family have also prayed for them. For years, we have waited, but in the waiting, I have found the hope to which I must cling.

The promise given to us in Isaiah 55:11 is that God's Word will never return void. When it goes out, it will accomplish what He intended it to accomplish. My intentions aside and God's intentions fulfilled is what this verse teaches me. God has never, nor does it seem that He will anytime in the near future, work according to my timetable. Thank goodness for that, right?

Rest is found while trusting God in the waiting.

Because He is slow to anger and abounding in steadfast love to all who would call on His name, His patience in His dealings with us is astounding. His wrath has every right to consume every last one of us, but His patience bears with us one day at a time. That is also true of those for whom we are praying. Every time God's Word has fallen on those lost ears, it has had a purposeful impact, whether we ever see the fruition of it or not. How do I know this to be true with such certainty? Because, God's Word never returns void. Every time you have shared the love of Jesus Christ with someone outside of faith, God's Word accomplished the purpose that it set out to do in that interaction. Trust that. Find hope in that.

If your hope is dwindling, and you feel that you may never see that one whom you love so dearly embrace Jesus Christ as Lord, and if you are tempted to throw in the towel on prayer, remember this:

As long as there is breath in their lungs, there is hope for their soul.

God hasn't given up on them, so why should you? Never stop praying. Never stop sharing. Never stop speaking truth. Never stop living redeemed. God's Word is alive and active, sharper than any double-edged sword, and it accomplishes absolutely EVERYTHING that it sets out to do. There is no match for the Word of God, not even the hardest of hearts or the unbelieving soul. Remain steadfast on your knees, standing in the gap for that one who is far from the heart of God. My hope is built on nothing less.

Rest is found while trusting God in the waiting.

My conviction from Day 11:

....
....
....
....
....
....
....
....
....
....

My prayer:

....
....
....
....
....
....
....
....
....

DAY 12
WHERE CAN I FIND
SOME PEACE?

"This is what the LORD says—your Redeemer, the
Holy One of Israel: 'I am the LORD your God, who
teaches you what is best for you, who directs you
in the way you should go. If only you had paid
attention to my commands, your peace would
have been like a river, your well-being like the
waves of the sea.'"

Isaiah 48:17-18

I wonder how many reading this today feel as if they are lacking
peace in life. I wonder how many doubt if peace, true peace,
will ever be afforded to them. I wonder how many of you have
prolonged decisions based on a lack of peace. I wonder if we have
ever linked our lack of peace to our lack of obedience. I wonder.

It has already been said and studied throughout this short, 30-day
devotional that God has commanded us to practice rest. It's not a
suggestion. It's a command. There is a responsibility on our part
to walk in obedience to what God has required of us. I wonder, yet
again, how many of us are lacking peace in our lives because we

have refused to prioritize obedience to this specific command that God has given us in His Word.

There have been many times in my own life when peace seemed so unattainable, so out of reach. Peace is something I've consistently prayed for and longed for in my life. Who doesn't want peace, right? Who isn't ready to get rid of some turmoil, worry, fear, and stress? I wish I could see how many of your hands are enthusiastically shooting up into the air right now and how many heads are nodding in agreement. We all want peace. We all need peace. So, where and how can we find it?

Let's start with the where. Galatians 5:22 tells us that peace is among the fruits of the Spirit. God is the giver and the sustainer of peace. Answering the question "where" is a no-brainer. It's the "how" that leaves us speechless at times. It's the "how" that leaves us wondering and doubting whether real peace actually exists and if we'll ever know it in our own lives. Let's look back at our verses today from Isaiah 48 to find our answer to the "how."

First, the prophet Isaiah unfolds in verse 17 what appears to be a reminder of God's résumé to his readers. Our first error we make in regards to lacking peace is forgetting who God says He is in His Word. We are reminded here that He is our Redeemer. He is Holy. He is capital "G" God. He wants what is best for us. He is our guide, showing us the way to go. It is upon that incredible foundation that we move to verse 18 which instructs us on "how" we can find peace, but also "why" we are lacking it.

I'm not sure why we have forgotten that peace is directly linked to obedience, but it appears that we have. God spells it out for us here in black and white. God is essentially saying to us, *"If you would have done what I told you to do, you would have abundant peace. Because you didn't, you don't have peace."* This is the message that this world needs to hear. We so quickly jump to point the finger of blame at God when things go wrong and when we find ourselves void of peace, but what about the responsibility that rests on our shoulders to walk in obedience to the commands that He has given us, commands that are for our good, protection, and blessing?

I imagine some of us came to the table of Bible study today hurting and broken, wounded from hard lives, and desperate for some relief. Know this: the peace that you desperately seek is found in Jesus Christ, and peace becomes reality in life when we purpose to walk in obedience to His commands—all of His commands. Our circumstances might not change, but our hearts and minds will. God wants you to have and to know His peace. Find it in Him and within the safety of the boundaries that He has set up for us in His Word.

Then, you will know peace. Then, you will have rest. Then, you will be satisfied.

My conviction from Day 12:

....

....

....

....

....

....

....

....

....

....

My prayer:

....

....

....

....

....

....

....

....

....

"Be still, and know that I am God; I will be exalted
among the nations, I will be exalted in the earth."

Psalm 46:10

DAY 13

Spend some time meditating on the passage and collage on the previous page. What do you see? What do you hear? Write a prayer of reflection below.

DAY 14
TO BE STILL IN A RACING WORLD

Maybe it's because I was born and raised in the church or maybe it's because of my tendency towards "full-plate" living, but I've always wondered at the tension between Psalm 46:10 and the insanely busy lives we lead.

"Be still, and know that I am God. I will be exalted among the nations, I will be exalted in the earth!"

Or maybe it's because the culture in which we live glorifies "busyness" to the degree that if you're not busy, something must be wrong. Right? We know this tension. We feel it every day. Someone asks you, "How have you been?," and how many times have you immediately replied, "Busy!"? It's almost an addiction. We crave busyness even if we complain about it, and when we find ourselves coming across a moment of stillness, we grab our phones and fill the space with the busyness of others' lives portrayed on social media.

What is that?!

Just recently, we had some family visiting us from Germany. I have always loved Germany, but perhaps one of my favorite things about it is the pace of life that exists there. It isn't rushed, not as it is here, anyway. They seem to prioritize "slow" in such a beautiful way. Here in America, our tendency is to fill our daily schedules with as much as possible, leaving little to no room for margin. Not so there. And the slower pace affords a sense of peace that is priceless.

Why is it so hard for us to be still? Why do we fight against it? We are quick to voice how exhausted we are when asked, but much slower to do anything about it. Why?

Perhaps, we fear the voice we will hear in the silence.

Make no mistake, God is always present, and He is always speaking to us, but the noise of our busy lives can quickly muffle out the sound of His voice. When we still ourselves and quiet ourselves before Him, we are inviting Him to speak directly to us, and unfortunately, some of us don't want to hear what He might have to say.

Because in the stillness, His voice is clear.

We can no longer conclude that we heard Him wrong or continue justifying the behaviors of our lives anymore when we quiet the noise of our lives long enough for Him to speak into it.

The invitation is clear. It is extended to you and me today. Be still. That's it. Because in the stillness comes a knowing. A knowing that He is God, and we are not. A knowing that all of our efforts to control and maintain our lives will never strip Him of His sovereignty. A knowing that the peace we are desperate for is afforded to us in His presence.

So, come today, friends. Come and sit at His feet. Come and rest. Come with the affections of your hearts, not the works of your hands. Rest is possible in this racing world, and He wants us to know it. In the stillness, His voice is clear. So, be still today.

My conviction from Day 14:

....

....

....

....

....

....

....

....

....

....

My prayer:

....

....

....

....

....

....

....

....

....

....

DAY 15
RESTING DURING THE URGENT

Have you ever stopped to wonder what it would have been like to be there when Jesus walked the face of this earth? What would it have been like to know Him, to travel from town to town with Him, to hear Him teach, and see Him heal the sick? How would it have felt to be in His inner circle of friends—to be the very ones at the foot of the cross, to dress His wounds in preparation for burial? I can only imagine.

We're able to read about the lives of many of those who found themselves side-by-side with Jesus throughout His life and even His death. What a wild ride it must have been! What faith it must have required to trust and follow Him! What grief and sorrow must have been experienced as He took His final breath on that cross. What tears must have flowed as they laid Him in that tomb.

As I studied "rest" throughout Scripture this past year, there were several passages that immediately came to mind without a second thought. The fascinating part of this journey for me, though, has been uncovering the portions of Scripture that speak to this Divine invitation to come rest that I would never have thought were related before. Today's verse is one of those hidden treasures for me. Here it is in all its splendor:

"Then they went home and prepared spices and perfumes. But they rested on the Sabbath in obedience to the commandment."

. . . .

Luke 23:56

The verse you just read falls into the storyline of the death, burial, and resurrection of Jesus Christ. Jesus' body had just been placed in the tomb, and it was customary for family and friends to prepare spices and perfumes for the body to help prevent odor as the body decayed. Not only was this an urgent matter, as you can imagine, but this was for Jesus. How much more urgent could this seem for His followers? I can only imagine wanting to do this right away without delay. I can only imagine wanting to be near Him one more time. I can only imagine feeling so compelled to provide this for Him at a time when all else probably seemed hopeless. Yet, we read something so moving in Luke 23:56. Rather than doing what they probably felt they wanted to do—rushing towards the urgent, the very thing calling their name, the "to-do" list—they obeyed the command to rest on the Sabbath.

I don't know about you, but I simply cannot imagine responding in such obedience as they did. I'm a rule-breaker, so maybe that's why, but I imagine I would have come up with a good excuse to get those spices and perfumes to Jesus. I would have resisted rest and rushed toward what seemed urgent, but they didn't. And this shouted something so clear to my soul.

I am repeatedly found bowing down to the urgent demands in my life, thus forfeiting the most important—time spent resting in His presence. Anybody else? For most of us, it's only a matter of minutes into our days before "urgent" needs begin to present themselves. We may have woken up that day with every intention to start things off right with Jesus, but then the phone rings, the kid screams, the milk spills, the emails come pouring in, and before we know it, the sun has set on another day, and we have gone without Sabbath. We have sacrificed rest for the urgent.

Please hear what I am not saying. I'm not saying rest is easy. I'm not even saying that it will always seem possible. I'm saying it's necessary, and I'm saying we have a choice. These women who loved Jesus and had followed Him for years made a decision that Sabbath morning. I'll bet you anything that they wanted to be at the tomb, ministering to the broken body of Jesus, but instead they obeyed. Instead, they rested, and I can't help but wonder what the product of that rest was. Was it an even greater eagerness and anticipation to rush to the tomb the following morning? Or was it the Divine message they received when they arrived at the tomb, that their Jesus was no longer there, but He had risen just as He had said?

What is the "urgent" in your life right now, the things that keep you on your feet, rushing from thing to thing and off your knees? What are the demands that push their way before and in front of the invitation to find rest in Jesus? Could you, today, press pause on the "urgent" in order to know the rest that God calls you to? Could you prioritize the most important over the urgent? Rest awaits you.

My conviction from Day 15:

....

....

....

....

....

....

....

....

....

....

My prayer:

....

....

....

....

....

....

....

....

....

DAY 16
IS YOUR PLATE TOO FULL?

It was probably a few years ago now that the Lord began convicting me about saying "yes" to everything—or maybe that's just when I started listening. I've always been someone who likes to have lots of plates spinning in the air. I love to be busy, and I function well, for the most part, at high capacity. Still, I would find myself burning out after extended periods of time, when I was found doing too much of everything.

The hard but necessary lesson that the Lord was trying to teach me then and now, is "how to say 'no' to good things so that I can say 'yes' to the best things." Why is this so hard to do? I imagine I'm not alone in this struggle, either. It may be quite easy for us to say "no" to things that don't interest us, but when a good opportunity comes along, how on earth do we say "no" to that?

The hamster wheel I was finding myself in was "the yes game." Every opportunity that came my way: "Yes!" Every person who needed my help: "Yes!" Every get-together with friends: "Yes!" Every speaking engagement: "Yes!" I think you get the picture. I have always found it very hard to say "no," especially to good things. Here is what I've learned, though—I cannot do all things well. It's not rocket science, right? You might even be laughing at me right now, but it was a hard reality that I had to come face to face with. When you and I say "yes" to everything that is presented to us, what we end up finding out (and usually the hard way) is that we are only able to do all things at about 50% instead of giving 100% of ourselves to it.

Because it's impossible to be everything to all people and to do all things well.

We're going to keep trying to, though, aren't we? We will exhaust ourselves in trying, but at the end of the day, we'll be left wondering why we did all of these great things and yet we still feel empty and worn out. This is where our passage comes into play for today. Here it is. Read it slowly, and soak it in.

"Now this is what the Lord Almighty says: "Give careful thought to your ways. You have planted much, but harvested little. You eat, but never have enough. You drink, but never have your fill. You put on clothes, but are not warm. You earn wages, only to put them in a purse with holes in it." This is what the Lord Almighty says: "Give careful thought to your ways."

Haggai 1:5-7

The first time I read those words, I felt as if they were written specifically for me. This is me on so many of my days—running around, doing so much, but harvesting nothing but exhaustion at the end of the day. This is not what the Lord would want for us. Do we ever pause for long enough before we commit ourselves to another thing to "give careful thought" to our ways? Or do we just say "yes" and determine to think about it later?

If we are to ever truly know rest, then we must start living by Haggai 1:5-7. There is wisdom in learning how to say "no." There is wisdom in setting healthy boundaries around your time and the things to which you commit yourself. There is wisdom in thinking and praying before deciding. There is wisdom in slow living. I can't help but wonder how much we forfeit rest in our lives simply because we do not stop for long enough to consider our ways.

For some of you, your plate may be full with two things, and for others, your plate may be full with seven. This isn't a lesson on finding the magic number of things we are allowed to commit ourselves to. This is a lesson about learning to bring all of our plans, dreams, desires, commitments, schedules, and everything else before the Lord first and taking a few moments to breathe in His wisdom before rushing into yet another thing that will fill our days. Do you feel as if you're pouring out far more than you're getting in return? Do you find yourself still hungry and thirsty even after you've had your fill? Does your labor seem to be in vain? Perhaps, your plate is too full. Perhaps, it is time to pause. Perhaps, it is time to start giving careful thought to your ways. Perhaps, you need a good dose of rest.

My conviction from Day 16:

....

....

....

....

....

....

....

....

....

....

My prayer:

....

....

....

....

....

....

....

....

....

....

DAY 17
BEAUTY IN THE MORNING

"Let the morning bring me word of your unfailing love, for I have put my trust in you. Show me the way I should go, for to you I entrust my life."

Psalm 143:8

I wonder how differently our days would be ordered if we began each one of them with the words of this prayer. It's the same thought that drives the words of this song, "In the morning, when I rise, give me Jesus." When we pull the covers back, place our feet on the hard, cold ground of life to start a new day, rub our tired eyes, and stretch our stiff limbs—in all of these things, are we even looking for glimpses of His beauty? Are we searching for Jesus when we wake?

Coffee seems to be the first thing on my mind when I get out of bed. You too? I'm so glad I'm in good company. A second confession I will wholeheartedly make today is that I rarely feel rested in the morning. To say that I'm not a morning person is quite possibly the understatement of the year. Stumbling down the stairs toward the coffee maker is always somewhat frightening for me, never knowing if I'm going to find myself tumbling down them until I'm nothing more than a heap on the floor at the bottom. The treacherous descent down those stairs always proves to be worth it though, as those first few sips of caffeine surge through my body, awakening my very soul it seems at times.

As I laugh to myself, thinking about the effect coffee has on me, I can't help but also think to the times when I found myself just as desperate for Jesus, just as weary, just as thirsty, just as weak, just as tired. Whenever I purpose to pursue Him, trusting that the strength I am so desperately seeking after will be found in Him, I find myself awakened to new life. That is the thrill of walking hand in hand with Jesus. That is the new life that He gives. What was dead comes to life. What was crumbling around me is made new in Him. When the world around me falls and fails me, my feet stand firm on the Rock of my salvation, the Rock who will not move. Hope is restored. Rest is regained.

As I made my way down those stairs once again this morning, and as I turned the corner that leads me to my beloved coffee pot, I was once again reminded of the words of Psalm 143:8.

Beauty in the morning.

Worship and gladness in the morning.

Trust in the morning.

The God of the Universe, who set the planets in motion and gave the sun, moon, and stars their light, is the same God who sustains my very life and offers my next breath. This same God gives life, vibrant color, and distinguished beauty to the flowers I can see outside my kitchen window. This is our God.

Open up your eyes. Look around you. Open up your heart. As much as there is calamity, disaster, and pain in this world, the light of Christ will always be more. His beauty radiates within His people and pours out in each gentle smile, through each warm

embrace, and in each patient and loving exchange. The light of
Christ overwhelms the darkness of this lost world every time we,
as God's children, choose to see beauty in the morning and praise
Him for it. Praise alters our moments and turns the course of
our days. Days that were once heading down the road of anger,
bitterness, and ingratitude can now be spent filled with wonder,
awe, and praise.

Open up your eyes. He is here. Breathe Him in. Breathe Him out.
In this awakening, find rest for your weary soul.

My conviction from Day 17:

....

....

....

....

....

....

....

....

....

....

My prayer:

....

....

....

....

....

....

....

....

....

....

DAY 18
GOD KNOWS WHAT HE'S DOING

"For my thoughts are not your thoughts, neither are your ways my ways, declares the LORD. For as the heavens are higher than the earth, so are my ways higher than your ways and my thoughts than your thoughts."

Isaiah 55:8-9

I remember the very first time I heard these verses read aloud. I was sitting across the table from a woman who had been walking with the Lord for years, far longer than the sum total of my own life. I sat quietly as I listened to her speak about her faith in God. I leaned in, and despite the numerous trials she had faced in life and the countless obstacles that she had overcome, she came back to these two verses with such a confidence in God's character that astounded me. As she shared, I could see deep roots of faith in her that had grown over years of trusting in this one truth:

God knows what He's doing.

I know that I'm not alone when I say that I struggle with always needing to know why things happen. I've always been this way. I've demanded the "why" behind the "what" for as long as I can remember, and quite frankly, this stubborn stance has often gotten me in trouble. We are a people who want answers to the unanswerable things in this life. Someone dies unexpectedly, and we demand for God to explain Himself. We receive the dreaded diagnosis, and we unashamedly point the finger of blame at God. We lose a job, and suddenly we are questioning the God of the Universe to give us a detailed explanation as to why He let this happen. Crisis erupts around us, and in our limited understanding of the bigger picture, we expect God to answer our every "why."

Although I fully believe that there are times when God does in fact answer the "whys" that we throw at Him, I can't help but think that He is far more interested in our "whats."

"God, what do you want me to learn from this?"

"Lord, what should I do in response to this?"

"Father, what part of me needs to change in order to trust you more through this?"

Of course, this is not the rule, but for the most part I think our "whys" reflect a deeper issue, a trust issue. Because we can't understand why, our willingness to trust God in it becomes increasingly difficult. Our insistent "whys" reveal a weakness in us. Our perspective is based off of a very limited view. We can only see a small portion of the greater picture and purpose of what God is doing in our lives and in the world around us.

However, if we could just take a step back from our circumstances and rest in the truth that Isaiah 55:8-9 provides, I believe we would find peace. If we could begin to ask "what" in place of "why," I believe we would begin to see heart change occur within us. If we could release our white-knuckled grip on our circumstances and approach God open-handed instead, the fear, worry, anxiety, and doubt just might be replaced with faith, peace, rest, and trust.

The person who asks "what" instead of "why" demonstrates a desire to trust the Lord who is in control, whose ways and thoughts are higher than our own—the God who knows what He is doing. There is rest to be found in this place. There is a release that occurs in trusting. There is faith that is deepened in shifting our gaze. Do you believe that Isaiah 55:8-9 is true? Do you believe that it is not only true for your neighbor, your friend, and your pastor, but it is also true for you, today? Do you believe that rest can be had and fully known in places of uncertainty? Do you believe that God sees the whole picture and is working all things out for the good? Do you believe that God is love and He knows what He is doing? Choosing to trust God brings us to places of rest. Be found in that place today.

My conviction from Day 18:

....

....

....

....

....

....

....

....

....

....

....

My prayer:

....

....

....

....

....

....

....

....

....

....

DAY 19
WHEN GOD IS SILENT

"How long, O LORD? Will you forget me forever?
How long will you hide your face from me?"

Psalm 13:1

If there was anyone who understood what God's silence sounded like it was King David, the man after God's own heart. Why? Because, David also knew the sound of God's voice so well. Chosen by God as a young boy to rule over Israel, defeater of Goliath the giant Philistine, writer of many of the Psalms, a victor in battle, and a true worshipper and lover of God, he certainly was acquainted with the sound of God's voice. So, can you imagine the ache in his heart and the longing of his soul when God appeared to have gone silent in his life? Can you imagine his desperation to be in God's presence once again? Pursued nearly unto death on multiple occasions, David remained steadfast in his devotion to the God of Israel. Although he was certainly not without fault, he never failed to return to the Lord in his time of need. His enemies hotly pursued him, and he poured out the cries of his heart to God in prayer.

Rest is found in thanksgiving.

David had a way with words. As you may already know if you've read the Psalms, the cries of David's heart are so beautifully penned in Scripture, in particular the Psalms that were written in his darkest hours. Psalm 13 displays an utter despair due to his current circumstances, and yet it somehow culminates in praise to a faithful God. How does he do that? When God is apparently silent in David's life causing him to cry out in desperation, how does David resort to praising God in the midst of his storm? How is it possible that David, who is in constant turmoil from the pursuit of his enemies, can offer praise and thanksgiving to the God who he has been striving to hear from and yet has failed to see present in his life?

Like David, I think each one of us can relate to seasons in our own lives when God has appeared to be silent. We cry out, and we hear nothing. We pray and petition for what seems in vain. How do we respond to His silence? How can we respond as David did? Perhaps, it's as simple as forming a habit of praise.

Rest is found in thanksgiving.

I tend to think that David formed such habits throughout his early years, and that was what enabled him to respond in such a way when it really mattered in his later years. How else could he approach Goliath with such confidence and boldness? How else could he enter into battle with such courage? He knew that the God of Israel went before him and was on his side. Therefore, he had a reason to praise. He had a reason for thanksgiving. If nothing else, he knew that God was his defender.

David was certain of whose he was, and so he acted accordingly. Therefore, when God fell silent in his life, David knew to rehearse His faithfulness. David was well-acquainted with the steadfast love and kindness of the Lord because he had experienced it on numerous occasions, as have you and I. He was able to still sing to the Lord because he chose to remember God's faithfulness to him in his past, and he chose to trust in the God who never changes. David refused to allow his shifting and changing circumstances to alter his understanding of God's unchanging character. Simply put, David had developed a habit of praise.

Rest is found in thanksgiving.

What habits have you formed in your relationship with God? Do you only approach Him with requests when things get tough? Or have you developed a habit of praising Him in both the good and the bad times? David set an excellent example for us all. He didn't stop crying out to God in his need, but he also didn't stop praising the God who deserved his praise despite his need.

Rest is found in thanksgiving.

My conviction from Day 19:

....

....

....

....

....

....

....

....

....

....

My prayer:

....

....

....

....

....

....

....

....

....

....

"For anyone who enters God's rest also rests
from their works, just as God did from His."

Hebrews 4:10

DAY 20

Spend some time meditating on the passage and collage on the previous page. What do you see? What do you hear? Write a prayer of reflection below.

....

....

....

....

....

....

....

....

....

....

....

....

....

....

....

....

DAY 21
WHAT REST REQUIRES

When you hear the word "rest," what is it that comes to mind? Do you immediately think of sleep? Does your mind go to your Sunday afternoon nap? Do you start to dream about vacation? What words or images come to mind when you think about what it means to "rest?" We've been at this for a few weeks now, so I hope you are getting to the place where you can begin to articulate what it means for you to rest.

As I've already mentioned, God has been wooing me, calling me out of the places of busyness and stressful living to places of rest with Him. That is exactly what these 30 days are all about. They are the overflow of what He has been teaching me this year.

While rest may sound ever so enticing to you, I have to confess that it has been much harder than I would have anticipated to follow Him obediently in this. I'm a busy person. I like to have a full plate. I enjoy a lot going on. I like to say "yes" to nearly everything that is asked of me. However, it had gotten to the point in my life where I was almost idolizing busyness. If I wasn't busy, I felt unaccomplished and unimportant. I was allowing busyness to define me. So, God in His mercy and firm love continues to call me away from that pursuit and back to the simplicity and beauty of pursuing Him above all else.

Today, I want to explore with you a passage in the book of Hebrews. Open your Bible to Hebrews 4, and take the next few minutes to read through the entire chapter. Go ahead. It's only 16 verses long.

This passage speaks often of rest and the importance of entering into God's rest. The original Hebrew reader would have been well-versed in Old Testament Law which commanded a Sabbath rest for all. You were required to work six days each week and to rest on the seventh, just as God did when He created the world. There is beauty in that. God modeled for us from the very beginning of time this important and necessary element of rest. God wasn't tired after creating for six days, but He knew we would be tired and would need a break from our own work. So, in His mercy and because of His love, He set a standard for rest.

Here's the interesting thing about rest. I find that we tend to either abuse it or refuse it. There's a fine line somewhere in the middle, but for the most part I've seen a tendency toward one extreme or the other. What would be an abuse of rest? When it's all play and little work, we abuse rest. When we shy away from responsibility because we prefer fun, we abuse rest. But then there is the refusal to rest. This would be represented best in the workaholic mentality. This is all work and no play. This is working on your days off. This is the absence of margin. This is not knowing when to stop.

To find the balance and the margin that Christ calls us to, we need to take a look at what rest requires. In order for us to steer clear of the abuse of rest and the refusal of rest, we need a biblical perspective of what God intended rest to be.

Rest requires discipline. It requires the commitment to give your all and to work as unto the Lord and not man (Colossians 3:23), but it also requires the ability to possess and maintain boundaries. It requires the ability to walk away and say "no" when "no" needs to be said. Discipline is not only knowing how and when to say "yes," but it's also knowing how and when to say "no."

Rest requires hard work. God didn't model laziness when He rested on the seventh day. He modeled wisdom. A hard week of work requires a day of rest. Likewise, true rest requires hard work. Rest is most restful when we have given our all and held nothing back. If we maintain the mentality that in all things we are working for the Lord, then hard work should be our natural default.

Finally, rest requires trust. To cease working for a day requires trust in the Lord that this world will keep on spinning and life as we know it will go on without my efforts for one day. This is a hard one for many of us. Every time our phone alerts us of another incoming email, our tendency is to jump to respond, is it not? But, there is wisdom in pausing. Rest trusts that God will provide in the absence of my own efforts. There is wisdom in choosing to rest after hard work. It requires trust, but rest is the reward.

My conviction from Day 21:

....

....

....

....

....

....

....

....

....

....

My prayer:

....

....

....

....

....

....

....

....

....

....

....

DAY 22
TO THOSE WHO ARE ABOUT TO GIVE UP

I recently sat in a room with a group of women who live faith-filled lives. What does that mean? Their lives probably mirror yours in many ways—family responsibilities, financial struggles, wayward children, faithless loved ones, good days, and bad. What is the thing that sets them apart in my eyes? They cling to Jesus as their hope and His Word as their guide. While this detail may seem small or insignificant to some, faith makes all the difference in the world.

The reality that struck me again is that we all face times of desperate need. Seasons of adversity are experienced by all. The faithful are not exempt from trial. As I sat and listened as some of these women shared what was going on in their lives through tears, I reflected on the times in my own life when my faith seemed to be wearing out. I can remember times when I felt like giving up would have been easier than continuing to run the race. But I am so glad that I clung onto the hands of Jesus.

To those who are about to give up, to anyone who is ready to throw in the towel, to the weary pilgrim who can't fathom taking one more step, to the one who is broken from life's crashing waves, to the tired mama and neglected wife, to the lonely and forgotten:

It only takes a mustard seed.

"Truly I tell you, if you have faith as small as a mustard seed, you can say to this mountain, 'Move from here to there,' and it will move. Nothing will be impossible for you."

Matthew 17:20

It only takes an admission.

"Immediately the boy's father exclaimed, "I do believe; help me overcome my unbelief!"

Mark 9:24

It only takes a prayer.

"Restore to me the joy of your salvation and grant me a willing spirit, to sustain me."

Psalm 51:12

I don't know where this finds you today, in the valley or on the mountaintop, but the hope you can know is that Jesus Christ created both, and both are His dwelling place. May God open your eyes to see His nearness in your pain. In your fight to hold on and remain faithful, remember that He fights harder for you than you ever could for Him, and no one can snatch you out of His hand.

To those who are about to give up:
New mercies await you in the morning.
Grace sufficient for the day is just around
the corner. Jesus loves you more than
you could fathom. Rest in this today.

My conviction from Day 22:

....
....
....
....
....
....
....
....
....
....

My prayer:

....
....
....
....
....
....
....
....
....
....

DAY 23
RESTING IN HIS PROVISION

I had a week recently that I will not soon forget. It began here in Arizona with the women of my church, whom I love, getting them excited and registered for this upcoming season of Bible studies—something that will never get old for me. My week then took me out to California to teach another group of women whom I have grown to love over the past few years. I have spent a large part of my summer with them, teaching them through the book of Ephesians, verse by verse. My week then took me to the shores of the San Diego beaches with two dear friends, both of whom I've known most of my life. The long trek back from the beach to the desert led me to my week's next highlight, as I got to reconnect with another dear friend from my college days. She was out here in Phoenix leading worship, so not only was I blessed to worship under her leadership, but our conversations throughout the day were truly life-giving.

All of that led me to the experience I had at the end of this epic week. A week filled with plans, busyness, and joy all served in one way or another to prepare me for what I had the privilege to do as my week came to a close. My church here in Arizona has a huge heart for foster care, so much so that they have created a space for foster parents to meet, to be encouraged, to build community with one another, and to receive the training and tools they need to keep walking this often difficult road. I was asked to speak to this group, and while I was so excited going into it, deeply desiring to bless and encourage them, I had no idea how blessed I was about to be from them in return.

The moment I stepped into the room, a humility washed over me like I've never experienced before. It was as if God were speaking directly to my heart about these people who have so bravely stepped out in faith to love the least of these. They have signed up for risk and have embraced sacrifice to the degree that I have not yet tasted, and I was honored but so humbled to share with them—a room filled with people who would never consider themselves heroes, but I most certainly would.

After I shared with them a word of encouragement to keep going and to not grow weary in doing good (Galatians 6:9), I had the opportunity to sit with several of them around a table and just hear their stories. They probably thought I was crazy because nearly the entire time, I bet my mouth was hanging open in shock and disbelief at some of the things they've faced and experienced on their own journeys with foster care. At one point, one of them grabbed my Bible and shared these verses with the small group at our table:

"A father to the fatherless, a defender of widows, is God in his holy dwelling. God sets the lonely in families,"

Psalm 68:5-6a

It was at that moment my heart swelled with faith. You see, not unlike the foster care system, much of our own lives can seem hopeless and a constant uphill battle at times. We struggle, we strive, we strain, and many times, we still seem to come up empty and lacking. As this faith-filled woman read the words from Psalm 68, I was reminded of God's provision. In this life, we will know lack. We will know hurt. We will know loss, sorrow, ache, and pain. But, in this life, if we are in Christ, we WILL also know His provision in the desert-like places of our lives. We WILL know His protection.

Because He is a good, good Father. It's just who He is. And we are loved by Him. It's just who we are. And despite how our circumstances try to inform us, they will never change the character of God. He remains the same. He remains the Father to the fatherless, the defender of the weak, our provider, and our protector.

Friends, there is rest to be found in this truth. There is a deep, soul rest to be found in this promise. There is unending rest to be found in His provision. He is a good Father. This is our God.

My conviction from Day 23:

....
....
....
....
....
....
....
....
....
....

My prayer:

....
....
....
....
....
....
....
....
....
....

DAY 24
THERE'S NO REST IN ANXIETY

Worry seems to come naturally to so many of us, doesn't it? If we could win an Olympic gold medal in worry and anxiety, many of us would have one. There is much in life to worry about. Much in this life causes anxiety. Much keeps us awake at night, robbing us of the peace that we so desperately need.

I love that Jesus was so practical in His teachings. He performed miracles, met very real needs, taught truth, and called out sin for what it is. In all of that, there was a practicality that spoke straight to human hearts. We can be taught all day long, but you and I both have a desire built within us to want to know what to do with that teaching. We want to be able to practically apply it to our lives. So did Jesus.

It shouldn't surprise a single one of us, then, that Jesus also addressed the issue that most human beings deal with on a daily basis: Anxiety. He not only addressed the issue, but He instructed us on how to rise above it and how to find rest and peace when it comes on strong like a tidal wave.

Take a few minutes to read through
Matthew 6:25-34.

Jesus begins His instruction with these powerful three words: "Do not worry …" Notice the imperative. It is not a suggestion. It's a command. This is interesting for me to think about because so often I feel as if I'm the victim of my own anxiety and worry. When life seems to get out of control and I can't determine which way is up, I feel as if there is no other option but to be anxious. Jesus knew we would be prone to this thinking, so He gave us some invaluable instruction on this. "Do not worry … ."

After taking a good, long, hard look at this passage, I couldn't help but walk away with this conviction: Fear is a choice. Worry is something that we decide to do. It is not forced upon us. We are the ones in control of our minds. We have the daily opportunity given to us to either choose faith or to choose fear, worry, and anxiety. Jesus would have never commanded us not to worry if it was an impossible thing to accomplish. He never said it would be easy, but rather, He said it is possible.

Another thing I absolutely love about the teachings of Jesus is that He never just leaves us with the command and walks away. Not only is further instruction given to us on how to obey, but we're also given a precious promise here in this passage. Let's start with the "how." This part has everything to do with our focus. Jesus goes on to say that we should consider the birds of the air and the flowers of the fields. He poses the rhetorical question, "Don't they have all that they need?" It's all a matter of focus and perspective. You see, what He is asking us to consider is that if He would go so far as to provide for the birds and the flowers, how much further would He go to provide for His children? The answer is "as far as it takes."

And there we have the promise. Take another look at Matthew 6:33. Notice the reminder given to us about focus. What are you looking at? Where are you looking to in order for your needs to be met? Jesus says, "Look to me. Seek me first." Then, the promise unfolds—"and all these things will be given to you as well." Don't miss this, friends. There is no lack for the devoted, Christ-seeking child of God. When we look to Him, our faces are radiant. When we seek Him above leaning on ourselves and our own understanding, we lack no good thing. When our focus is in the right place, there is no need to worry or fear.

Anxiety can be a thing of our past. It should be a thing of our past if we are in Christ. What we focus on is what we elevate in our minds. What we elevate in our minds is what we are tempted to worship. Sounds weird, doesn't it, that we would worship anxiety? Think about it, though. The more we focus on what causes us worry and anxiety, the less we are capable of focusing on Jesus Christ, our Provider. The less we focus on Him, the less we worship Him. The less we worship Him and are found in His presence, the less we know rest.

Friends, the invitation remains today. Find rest in God alone. There's no rest in anxiety. There's no rest in worry. The heavy weight that accompanies worry is lifted when we redirect our gaze to the face of Jesus. When we look to Him and seek Him first, all needs are met. Rest is had. So, lay down the burden of worry and anxiety, and in exchange, grab ahold of His extended hand that reaches out to you today.

My conviction from Day 24:

....

....

....

....

....

....

....

....

....

....

My prayer:

....

....

....

....

....

....

....

....

....

....

DAY 25
THE DISCIPLINE
OF FOCUS

"And the twelve summoned the full number of
the disciples and said, 'It is not right that we
should give up preaching the word of God to
serve tables.'"

Acts 6:2

I'll start by saying that it's best for you and me to read the above verse
in its context. I just gave you a little teaser for our topic today, but we
need the entire passage to understand the principle we will seek to
apply to our lives.

Take a quick minute right now to read Acts 6:1-7.

In short, the apostles were presented with a challenge, and a
significant one at that: distributing food to all of the widows in
their faith community, which more than likely numbered at least
1,000 women. The fact that they turned this service down in no way
signified that it was unimportant. On the contrary, they realized that

it was so important that they assigned seven qualified men to oversee this need. Why? How was it OK that they said "no" to meeting this need themselves? It is because they were called to focus on what God had asked them to do: prayer and the ministry (teaching) of the Word.

There's a whole lot that we could unpack from these seven short verses in the book of Acts, but today I just want to narrow it down to one main thing:

FOCUS

Did you realize that focus is a discipline? It's hard for us to say "no" to good things so that we can say "yes" to great things. Many good things in this life vie for our time and attention, but when these good things overtake the best things, the things that we must prioritize over all else, we've lost our focus.

For example, let's just look back at the text in Acts. The apostles had a significant need that had to be met. Widows were going without their daily distribution of food. They needed to eat. This job was noble and worthy of time and attention, just not their time and attention. Why? Because God had given them their priorities, which were prayer and the teaching of His Word. Had they allowed this urgent need to distract them from their primary calling, verse 7 might have been written quite differently. Instead, they appointed able men to address the need, and they were then freed to *FOCUS* on their priorities, which resulted in growth in the church.

What prioritizes your attention and your time? Is it what God has called you to or is it other pressing, urgent things that, although they may be good, are keeping you from fulfilling your primary purpose?

If you are married, one of your primary, God-given purposes is to love and prioritize your spouse. If you are single, one of your primary God-given purposes is to love and serve the people that God has placed in your life. Where we tend to get off course is when we fill our plates with everything that is good and leave little to no room for what is best. In this filling of our plates, we most often eliminate rest.

The discipline of focus recognizes and discerns the difference between good and best. The discipline of focus sees the value in pursuing and prioritizing the best in order to be the most effective. This goes directly against the mentality that much of our world embraces of "a mile wide but only an inch deep." How about we strive for depth more than width so that wherever we stake ourselves in the ground, we will find that we are deeply effective and purposeful. How about we discipline our focus so that we can begin to prioritize rest once again?

My conviction from Day 25:

....

....

....

....

....

....

....

....

....

....

My prayer:

....

....

....

....

....

....

....

....

....

....

DAY 26
EVER FEEL LIKE YOUR LABOR IS IN VAIN?

I imagine I'm not alone in this, but would you indulge me here for just a moment? Have you ever felt as if you've poured out every ounce of yourself but to no avail? When is the last time you worked so hard toward something or someone, and still came up empty or lacking? A chasing after the wind? An uphill climb without ever summiting that mountain? Do you ever feel as if your labor is in vain?

As you ponder how you would answer those questions, I'd like to welcome you to Jeremiah chapter two. Find your Bible, and meet me there.

Recently, in the different Bible study groups I lead, I taught on some hard truths—the honest truth—without sugar-coating it. While these lessons are seldom easy to hear and swallow (and let's be honest, far more difficult to teach), they are necessary. Why?

Sometimes, we need the sobering reminder of
the consequences of sin.

Yes, God's mercy covers. Yes, God's forgiveness redeems, but neither erases or eliminates the very real consequences that result from our sinful choices. This is the hard truth. This is what we more often than not need to hear but don't.

If you're not familiar with the Old Testament prophet Jeremiah, allow me to introduce you to him. He is referred to as the weeping prophet because he witnessed with his own eyes the brutal fall of God's chosen people and the aftermath of the destruction of God's house, and in short, it broke his heart. His consistent message and repeated plea to the nation of Israel was to repent—to turn from their wickedness and to run back to their God. But they just wouldn't.

Israel was determined to run after filth. They were determined to do things their own way, despite the warnings of inevitable punishment and despite the stories from their past. They chose evil again and again and again. Welcome to Jeremiah chapter two.

Jeremiah begins with remembrance—how Israel used to be faithful to God. However, after only four short verses, he quickly moves to rebuke.

"This is what the LORD says: 'What fault did your ancestors find in me, that they strayed so far from me? They followed worthless idols and became worthless themselves.'"

Jeremiah 2:5

Notice their singular downfall: idolatry. The moment they chose to put created things of this world before the Creator of this world, they became worthless, just like their idols. They removed God from the thrones of their hearts, and He, therefore, removed their effectiveness. Did you miss that? Take a look at the last three words of Jeremiah 2:5 again: *"became worthless themselves."* What once had been an effective nation, suddenly became worthless, ineffective, and futile, not to mention, captive. Why? Because they took their eyes off of God.

This story, although ancient in its context, bleeds principle into our lives today. What efforts are you making in this life? Are you seeking to climb the corporate ladder? Are you striving to have the best home and the most perfect children? Are you aiming to please everyone around you? And at what cost? God's Word makes it very clear from its opening story to its closing words:

We were created to worship.

The object of our worship was always intended to be our Creator, but we easily replace Him with the pressing and the urgent of our day to day lives. The reality is that we are going to worship something. The question is, "Who or what will we be found worshiping?" What is pressing and urgent in your life right now? What are you laboring after, and are you coming up empty?

"My people have committed two sins: They have forsaken me, the spring of living water, and have dug their own cisterns, broken cisterns that cannot hold water."

Jeremiah 2:13

Is God no longer #1 in your life? *"They have forsaken me."*

What cisterns are you digging? On what do you spend most of your time, energy, and resources? *"They have dug their own cisterns, broken cisterns that cannot hold water."*

Do you ever feel like your labor is in vain? Maybe it is. Maybe it's time for a turning from sin (repentance) and a returning to the One who created you to worship Him alone (reconciliation). Perhaps, it's time to turn from the busyness and the pursuit of all that you've deemed #1, and turn to finding all that you need in Jesus. There is a time for work, and there is a time for rest. We err when we only focus on the former, thus eliminating the latter.

My conviction from Day 26:

My prayer:

Read Psalm 23

DAY 27

Spend some time meditating on the passage and collage on the previous page. What do you see? What do you hear? Write a prayer of reflection below.

DAY 28
WHY PSALM 23 NEVER GETS OLD

I can't help but think that many, if not most of you have read the 23rd Psalm at some point in your life. You may even have it memorized. It's arguably one of the most quoted, referenced, and known passages in Scripture. I love the 23rd Psalm. I've read it more times than I could ever count, and over the years, I have become so familiar with its words.

"The Lord is my shepherd ..." Can you finish that sentence?

BUT...

With familiarity and repetition, has its impact faded or its words lost their luster? I've run in church circles for most of my life. I've heard all the talk. I've sung all the songs. I've memorized all the go-to passages. I know the drill. Anybody else? It's a slippery slope, really, and if we're not careful, we make God's grace and love less than commonplace when they are no less than miraculous and extraordinary.

So how do we avoid this numbing of our spiritual senses? I would suggest that all it takes is a deeper look, a slowing down, a pause, a pondering of the truths packed within the few short verses of this age-old Psalm.

"The Lord is my shepherd; I shall not want."

If you believe this to be true, then you'll truly know contentment. Because for all those who choose to make Christ their shepherd, they know no lack. They rest in places of contentment knowing that they have all they need in Him alone.

"He makes me lie down in green pastures. He leads me beside still waters. He restores my soul."

If you believe this to be true, then you'll truly know rest. True rest, soul rest. A deeper rest than sleep itself could ever provide. This promised rest is an absence of fear and anxiety. It is an assurance of restoration. It is tangible peace.

"He leads me in paths of righteousness for His name's sake."

If you believe this to be true, then you'll truly know and experience His guidance in your life. When you reach a fork in the road, because you've chosen to make the Lord your shepherd, you'll default to seeking His wisdom instead of operating in your own understanding. You'll trust in His leadership. You'll walk willingly down the paths He has prepared for you.

"Even though I walk through the valley of the shadow of death, I will fear no evil, for you are with me; your rod and your staff, they comfort me."

If you believe this to be true, then you'll know His protection. Protection provides a comfort, a peace, and ultimately, a rest that often eludes us in this life. When the Lord is your shepherd, the promise of His protection rests upon your life. This is not the promise of a worry-free, pain-free life. Rather, it's the promise of His constant presence with you no matter what perils you face.

"You prepare a table before me in the presence of my enemies; you anoint my head with oil; my cup overflows."

If you believe this to be true, then you'll truly know joy—the overflow of the obedient life. Because we have all but eliminated margin from our lives anymore, there tends to be little to no overflow. We live in places of burnout and exhaustion. However, when the Lord is your shepherd, the overflow of joy spills out into every aspect of your life because you've chosen to make Him the source of your strength.

"Surely goodness and mercy shall follow me all the days of my life, and I shall dwell in the house of the LORD forever."

Finally, you'll know and live in His favor. To know with certainty where your eternity lies offers a peace and a confidence that nothing else in this world could provide. God's favor rests upon the lives of those who choose to make Him Lord over them.

This is why Psalm 23, the entire counsel of God's Word, and community with His people never get old to me. Because there is always a stillness in His presence that is lacking elsewhere in life, even in the places with which I thought I was most familiar.

My conviction from Day 28:

....

....

....

....

....

....

....

....

....

My prayer:

....

....

....

....

....

....

....

....

....

DAY 29
WHEN LIFE IS HARD, GOD SPEAKS

There seem to be times in life when I perceive a greater need for God's Word. Maybe it's because when life gets hard, I'm more apt to run to Jesus than when things are going well. It's not to say that I need His Word any less in the days, weeks, and months when all seems to be going well, but I have found that His promises have been life and breath to me in my darkest hours.

When you find yourself in a difficult place, when life gets hard, where do you turn? To whom do you run? When all seems well and life appears to be without thorns and thistles, our perceived need for God withers, does it not? When we're not desperate, we cry out less. It's in those seasons of blessing that God often whispers into our hearts, and all the good and the blessings tune out the faint sound of His voice.

Perhaps you've heard this suggested to you before, but I believe it to be true with all of my heart. *God shouts in our pain.* It's not as if He hasn't been by our side all along speaking to our hearts, but I believe He uses the difficulty of life to increase our awareness of our need for Him. When life gets hard, God speaks into the pain. He speaks into the hurt. He speaks into the confusion. He speaks into the despair. Are you listening?

Rest is found in the sound of God's voice.

God speaks to us through His Word. He reveals His heart, His character, and His promises to us throughout the pages of Scripture. I find great comfort in meditating on His Word, and I receive a peace that cannot be attained elsewhere.

"My comfort in my suffering is this: Your promise preserves my life."

Psalm 119:50

Rest is found in the sound of God's voice.

God speaks tender words of love over us as His children through the truth found in His Word. His promises are true. You won't find empty promises in Scripture. He fulfills every promise that He makes. There is none like Him.

"Your Word, O LORD, is eternal; it stands firm in the heavens. Your faithfulness continues through all generations; you established the earth, and it endures."

Psalm 119:89-90

Rest is found in the sound of God's voice.

When life gets hard, we tend to remember the joy found in God's green pastures. It's then that we come running, in need of what we know can only be found in Him. We recall His goodness and the sweetness of His presence, and we long to be found there again. We must get to the place where that longing remains, even when life is good. Because even though our circumstances shift and change like the waves of the sea, God remains the same. He's always good. His presence is always sweet. His love never fails. Would we but remember that, our paths would be far less crooked.

"How sweet are your words to my taste, sweeter than honey to my mouth! I gain understanding from your precepts; therefore I hate every wrong path."

Psalm 119:103-104

Rest is found in the sound of God's voice.

God speaks as our defender when all else condemns and accuses us. He is our rock and our shield, a defense against our enemies that would pursue us and seek to destroy us. Hope can be found! Hope can be had! A shelter from the storm, this is our God.

"You are my refuge and my shield; I have put my hope in your Word."

Psalm 119:114

Rest is found in the sound of God's voice.

When life is hard, God speaks. Are you listening? Do you cling to His Word, knowing that the truth within will set you free? Are you crying out to Him, seeking Him in your pain? Where is your focus? Only the LORD can bring the quiet and still to your storm.

"I call with all my heart; answer me, O LORD, and I will obey your decrees. I call out to you; save me and I will keep your statutes. I rise before dawn and cry for help; I have put my hope in your Word."

Psalm 119:145-147

Rest is found in the sound of God's voice.

My conviction from Day 29:

My prayer:

DAY 30
DON'T GIVE UP

Allow me to just preface today's devotion with one foundational statement: We don't know true rest because we have taken our eyes off of Jesus.

I recently had the opportunity to have a Bible study with some of my closest girlfriends. These women are the female half of our small group that meets weekly, and we decided to just have a girls' night for Bible study this time. We got together in my living room, snacked on some yummy and healthy eats, and dove head first into Hebrews 12:1-3. Our conversation was riveting. We shared our struggles, we reflected back on times when we felt ever so close to God and celebrated those times, we prayed for each other, we cried, and we laughed. It was excellent. Even the hard was so good. Read the passage for yourself:

"Therefore, since we are surrounded by such a huge crowd of witnesses to the life of faith, let us strip off every weight that slows us down, especially the sin that so easily trips us up. And let us run with endurance the race God has set before us. We do this by keeping our eyes on Jesus, the champion who initiates and perfects our faith. Because of the joy awaiting him, he endured the cross, disregarding its shame. Now he is seated in the place of honor beside God's throne. Think of all the hostility he endured from sinful people; then you won't become weary and give up."

Hebrews 12:1-3

There it is in the New Living Translation, the text for our time together. As we unpacked each verse, we answered three questions. First, "what keeps your eyes on Jesus?" Since we're given the phrase "keeping our eyes on Jesus" in verse two, we figured it was a fairly important issue to address. How do we maintain a Christ-centered focus in a world that is focused on anything and everything but Him? What keeps our gaze on His face and off our problems? How would YOU answer this question?

Next, we moved to this question: "What takes your eyes away from Jesus?" We don't even have to try anymore to get caught up in the world. Temptation lurks around every corner trying to ensnare us—time spent on Facebook instead of in God's Word, an obsession with reality TV shows instead of being present with our families and developing "real" relationships with our neighbors, lust and perversity instead of purity and holiness. I mean, for real, when didn't it take a conscious effort on our part to keep our eyes on Christ? And therein lies the problem. We've stopped trying. We've stopped prioritizing Him. We've stopped starving the flesh in order to feed the spirit. How would YOU answer that question? "What takes your eyes away from Jesus?"

Finally, we settled in on verse three—"then you won't become weary and give up." And we hurt on this one. We cried. We ached and asked God, "Why?" Because life is hard. Because we are tired. Because our strength has failed us, and it is hard to raise that shield of faith when our faith seems to have worn thin. There are days when the temptation to give up is fierce. So, we answered the question, "What, right now, is making you weary and tempting you to give up?" How would YOU answer that question?

Here's the beauty, though. We didn't end there. I told you we discussed our answers to three questions, but after sharing our hearts on question #3, we ran right back to our focus. What are we looking at? Are we focused on our circumstances or the face of Jesus? Because when all we do is focus on our problems, our problems become pretty big, and our God becomes really small.

The strength you and I need to raise that shield of faith back up high in the air is not found within ourselves. It's found in Christ alone. So, we turn back to Him when our gaze has drifted from His face. We run back to Him when our feet have wandered from His pastures. We lean into Him when we've exhausted ourselves from pursuing everything else. We don't give up. We don't quit. We don't stop now. Because Heaven is but a breath away. Hold on, friends. Stretch out your arms and reach for the edge of His garment. Just a touch is all you need to heal. Don't give up. Press on. Rest returns to our lives as a known reality when our eyes are fixed on the face of Jesus. Victory comes when we don't give up.

My conviction from Day 30:

My prayer:

NeueThing.org

24859206R00075

Made in the USA
San Bernardino, CA
09 October 2015